SOUNDS AND SYMBOLS

Literacy through Music

Sounds and Symbols provides 'literacy-through-music' programmes
for pre-school children, primary school children and even adults!

Sounds and Symbols is dedicated to the promotion
of literacy skills through musical activities.

www.soundsandsymbols.co.uk

Building a sound foundation for literacy success!

Alphabet Book ^{+ More!}

Maria Kay

Illustrated by Aleksandra Karp

BKP
Bryant & Kay Publishing

Original illustrations by Aleksandra Karp

First published 2014

by Bryant & Kay Publishing

Fochabers, Scotland

ISBN 978-1-910102-00-8

Dedication

This book is dedicated to Grace MacKenzie,
the founder member of Sounds and Symbols in Elgin, Scotland

Acknowledgments

I would like to thank all my family for their help and support, without which, of course none of this book would be completed. I am indebted to them immensely.

Also thanks to Lizzie Sharp of Sharp Music Services, for her unfailing ability to interpret my musical requests!

About the Author and Illustrator

Author

Maria Kay is an experienced teacher and literacy practitioner.
She is also the founder of Sounds and Symbols (1998).

Illustrator

Aleksandra Karp is a fine arts graduate with a specialisation in graphic design. She has a great love of painting which you can appreciate here through her beautiful illustrations. You can see more of her work in her blog http://olakarp.blogspot.co.uk

Contents   Page

Introduction

This richly illustrated alphabet book offers the reader much more than just attractive alphabet characters. It was produced originally as a resource for the Sounds and Symbols literacy-through-music programmes for pre-school children. The Sounds and Symbols programmes use musical activities to foster the development of literacy skills. Likewise, this book includes a rhyme/song to accompany each letter of the alphabet and also suggests a song for singing the vowels. Music can assist the learning process and it's great fun too!

The 'Sounds and Symbols Alphabet Book + More', can be used to assist the development of all the elements of literacy – speaking, listening, reading and writing. It is multi-sensory, using sight, sound and touch to scaffold learning. The vibrant colours and effective shading help to maintain children's attention and help them to focus on the letter shapes and associated pictures.

Please enjoy reciting and singing the rhymes, admire the unique watercolours and use this book to build a sound foundation for literacy success for the next generation.

Early Literacy Skills

Whilst speech is innate, reading and writing are not. In order to become proficient readers, children must develop many skills. They need –

- a good command of spoken language and a rich vocabulary
- an appreciation that language can be represented by text
- an awareness of rhythm
- an ability to recognise rhyme
- an ability to recognise shape
- an awareness of variation in speech sounds
- comprehension of language and
- an understanding of sequence and ability to predict what might come next.

You can foster the development of each of the above by reading through this book with your child, encourage them to read too. On each page the letter of the alphabet is incorporated in the rhyme below it. Reciting rhymes helps children to recognise and subsequently, match sounds.

Emphasising rhythms helps children to detect syllables in words and increases their awareness of sound.

Emphasise rhythms when singing, by clapping hands or tapping claves. For example, 4 claps for alligator - al/li/ga/tor.

Regular activities are habit forming. Read frequently with your child and help them to recognise letter shapes and repeat letter sounds so that recall becomes automatic.

How Do Children Learn to Read?

Learning to read is a complex process. There are many factors which contribute to a child's success in this area. Looking through books is a first step to learning how books work; the direction of print and understanding that images and print can convey meaning. Children often learn to read environmental print such as notices, advertisements, grocery labels, road signs and logos before they start school.

At school or nursery, children may be taught phonics – a method of teaching reading where each letter of the alphabet has a sound which is blended with other letter sounds to make a word, 'd-o-g' for example. This method offers an excellent basis upon which further reading skills can be taught.

Not all words are spelt phonetically so children also need to learn some words by sight such as 'said'. This second method is referred to as 'whole word', 'look-say' or 'sight'. Children also need to learn that strings of letters 'ight' for example, can have the same sound. This is why it is important that children are able to match rhyming words. The string 'ite' also has the same sound as 'ight' and children need to know which string to use in different words.

A third method is that of using the context of the writing to determine what words might come next. For example, 'The lady had to use a torch when she went outside in the middle of the xxxxx. 'The information in the beginning of the sentence leads to reader to predict that the last word could be 'night'. Competent readers use context all the time and in fact do not 'read' every word on a page to derive meaning from text.

Using Music to Develop Literacy

The importance of sound to early reading cannot be overstated. Music can provide an excellent vehicle for learning about the sounds in language. Musical experience helps children to focus on variations in sound and helps to develop children's listening skills and concentration.

There are many common skills between those learned in early music sessions and those required for literacy. Some of them are listed below:

- Listening
- Imitation
- Rhythm
- Matching sounds – for example, initial sounds and rhyming endings
- An awareness of pitch - this is correlated with good reading skills
- Good communication skills – fluent speech and rich vocabulary, awareness of correct language sequencing.
- Appreciation of pattern
- Ability to relate sounds to symbols
- Visual discrimination – identification of shapes
- Co-ordination - being able to use both sides of the body effectively – one supporting the other
- Memory

When considering this list it is easy to see how musical activities can support the development of literacy skills. These areas are discussed in detail in the book, 'Sound Before Symbol – Developing Literacy through Music', along with many activity ideas. Further details can be found at the end of this book.

An obvious choice for linking music and learning about the alphabet is the well-known Alphabet Song (singing the letter names in order). This is often sung to the traditional tune of 'Twinkle Twinkle Little Star'. This can help children to remember the letter names and also the sequence of the alphabet letters. Music assists memory retention; many of us, as adults, can remember songs we learned long ago.

The rhyme on each alphabet letter page in this book, helps to reinforce that each letter has an associated sound. The rhyme is 'What Does This Letter Say?'

The song is a variation of the traditional tune for 'Skip to My Lou'. A backing track for this song can be downloaded from www.soundsandsymbols.co.uk.

There is also a song included which can be used to help learn the vowels – 'Five Vowels in the Alphabet'.

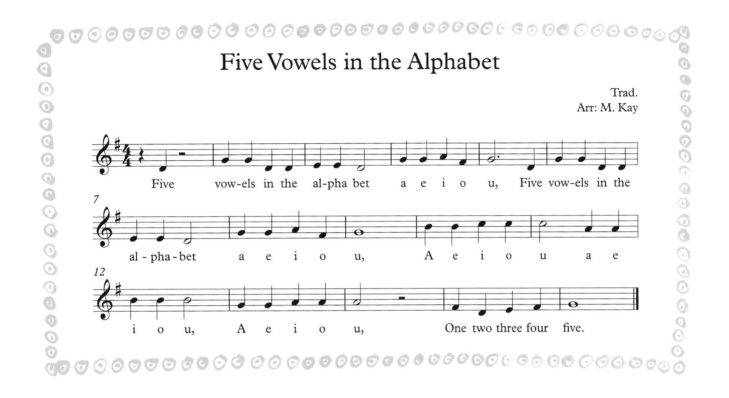

The song is a variation of the traditional tune for 'B-I-N-G-O'. A backing track for this song can also be downloaded from www.soundsandsymbols.co.uk.

You can sing the song using the vowel names or the vowel sounds.

Using music helps to consolidate language learning as it stimulates the brain, assists memory and helps vocalising to be more fluent. Music also adds a fun element and aids relaxation, thus creating an environment conducive to learning.

How to Give Your Child a Head Start

- Read and say the letter name of each letter as you point to it in the book. Remember that the upper and lower case letters have the same name. You can tell children there are big and small letters such as 'big A' and 'little a'.

- Each letter has a sound associated with it; pose the question 'What does an A say?' In the same way as you would ask 'What does a cow say?' Children soon make this analogy.

- Encourage children to draw round the letters with a finger. The starting point is indicated by a dot and the direction for writing the letter is indicated by arrows.

- The dotted line beneath each set of letters represents a line on lined paper and shows how the letter is positioned. Some letters, p or q for example, are written through the line, whilst others rest upon it. Help your child to be aware of this.

- For each letter there are three illustrations, depicting a word with the initial letter sound. The words are also written alongside. Point to the word alongside each picture as you read it.

- Encourage your child to read the words aloud too.

- When telling children that 'a' is for 'ant' make sure that you use the sound of 'a' not the letter name. Help your child to think up other words with the same initial sound.

- The syllables in each word are indicated by a coloured dot beneath them. Help children to identify these chunks of sound by clapping out the syllables as they say the words.
  For example, there are three syllables in 'croc/o/dile', two in 'ap/ple'.

- You can tap out the syllables of each word in the song as you sing along too to further reinforce learning. Tapping along to the rhythms of any song helps children to learn about syllables.

- Show children that each word is also made up of a series of sounds. For example, 'cat' has one syllable but three letter sounds c-a-t.

- By watching others read, children become readers themselves; let children know when you are reading newspapers, notices, information leaflets for example. Show children how books work, how to turn the pages; that books and print are read left to right and top to bottom. This is not the same for all languages.

- Spend time talking and communicating with your child. Use this book to initiate conversations. For example, the letter 'N' has a picture of a nose. Ask your child 'What can you smell?', 'What smells do you like?', 'What smells bad?', 'Where is your nose?'

- At the beginning and end of the book is an illustration of all the alphabet letters. There are four pictures also included. Ask your child which letter matches the initial sound for the name of each picture.

- Use the rhyme/song on each page to help your child to learn the letter sounds.

- After all the alphabet letters in this book, there is a set of vowels. These may be used for teaching initial letter sounds or for showing children how to blend letters together to make a word. The pictures may be used to illustrate how the vowels are sounded in the middle of a word – c-a-t, h-e-n, p-i-g, d-o-g, d-u-ck.

- Sing 'Five Vowels in the Alphabet' from page 7 to help your child to consolidate their learning of the vowel names and sounds.

Have fun with the alphabet pages!

The Letters of the Alphabet

ant

apple

What does this letter say?
Hey, hey, can anybody play?
What does this letter say?
This letter says 'a'.

arm

Bb

bag

book

What does this letter say?
Hey, hey, can anybody play?
What does this letter say?
This letter says 'b'.

bed

13

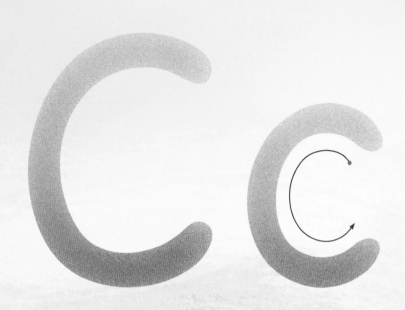

cat

crocodile

What does this letter say?
Hey, hey, can anybody play?
What does this letter say?
This letter says 'c'.

car

dog

doll

duck

What does this letter say?
Hey, hey, can anybody play?
What does this letter say?
This letter says 'd'.

egg

envelope

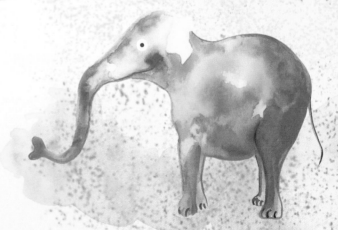

elephant

What does this letter say?
Hey, hey, can anybody play?
What does this letter say?
This letter says 'e'.

fan

fish

What does this letter say?
Hey, hey, can anybody play?
What does this letter say?
This letter says 'f'.

fork

goat

ghost

What does this letter say?
Hey, hey, can anybody play?
What does this letter say?
This letter says 'g'.

gate

hat

hand

What does this letter say?

Hey, hey, can anybody play?

What does this letter say?

This letter says 'h'.

horse

I i

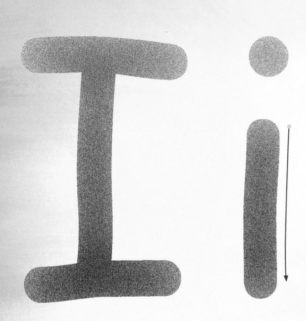

What does this letter say?

Hey, hey, can anybody play?

What does this letter say?

This letter says 'i'.

Indian

ink

igloo

jam

jigsaw

What does this letter say?
Hey, hey, can anybody play?
What does this letter say?
This letter says 'j'.

jug

kite

key

What does this letter say?

Hey, hey, can anybody play?

What does this letter say?

This letter says 'k'.

kangaroo

lamp

ladder

What does this letter say?

Hey, hey, can anybody play?

What does this letter say?

This letter says 'l'.

lion

milk

mouse

What does this letter say?

Hey, hey, can anybody play?

What does this letter say?

This letter says 'm'.

map

net

nose

What does this letter say?

Hey, hey, can anybody play?

What does this letter say?

This letter says 'n'.

neck

owl

orange

octopus

What does this letter say?

Hey, hey, can anybody play?

What does this letter say?

This letter says 'o'.

P p

pan

pen

panda

What does this letter say?

Hey, hey, can anybody play?

What does this letter say?

This letter says 'p'.

27

Qq

why?

question

queen

quilt

What does this letter say?

Hey, hey, can anybody play?

What does this letter say?

This letter says 'q'.

rain

R r

robot

What does this letter say?

Hey, hey, can anybody play?

What does this letter say?

This letter says 'r'.

rope

S s

sun

socks

sandwich

What does this letter say?

Hey, hey, can anybody play?

What does this letter say?

This letter says 's'.

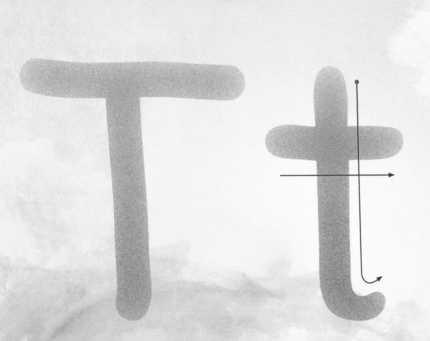

tooth

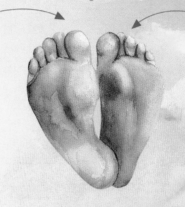
toes

What does this letter say?
Hey, hey, can anybody play?
What does this letter say?
This letter says 't'.

tiger

up

umbrella

under

What does this letter say?

Hey, hey, can anybody play?

What does this letter say?

This letter says 'u'.

violin

van

What does this letter say?

Hey, hey, can anybody play?

What does this letter say?

This letter says 'v'.

volcano

33

W w

What does this letter say?
Hey, hey, can anybody play?
What does this letter say?
This letter says 'w'.

wall

watch

whale

fox

box

What does this letter say?
Hey, hey, can anybody play?
What does this letter say?
This letter says 'x'.

x-ray

yoyo

yoghurt

yacht

What does this letter say?

Hey, hey, can anybody play?

What does this letter say?

This letter says 'y'.

Z z

zebra

zigzag

zip

What does this letter say?

Hey, hey, can anybody play?

What does this letter say?

This letter says 'z'.

The Vowels

There are five vowels in the alphabet. Each has a long sound and a short sound.

	Long	(as in the letter name)	Short
A	face		tap
E	evil		peg
I	mice		lid
O	hole		mop
U	flute		mug

Most words in the English language contain at least one vowel or a vowel sound. Sometimes the letter 'y' will take the vowel sound 'i' such as in 'sky', 'rhythm', 'gym'.

Sing 'Five Vowels in the Alphabet' which can be found on page 7.

What is the name and the sound of this vowel? Find the vowel in the word below the picture.

Can you sound out each letter in the word to read the name of the animal below?

Cat

What is the name and the sound of this vowel? Find the vowel in the word below the picture.

Can you sound out each letter in the word to read the name of the animal below?

Hen

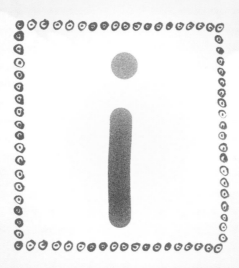

What is the name and the sound of this vowel? Find the vowel in the word below the picture.

Can you sound out each letter in the word to read the name of the animal below?

Pig

41

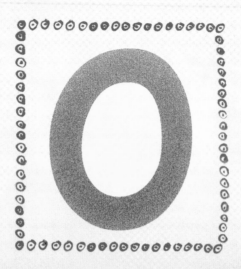

What is the name and the sound of this vowel? Find the vowel in the word below the picture.

Can you sound out each letter in the word to read the name of the animal below?

Dog

What is the name and the sound of this vowel? Find the vowel in the word below the picture.

Can you sound out each letter in the word to read the name of the animal below?

Duck

43

More Resources from Maria

'Sound Before Symbol – Developing Literacy through Music' by Maria Kay provides a thorough investigation of the role music may play in the development of literacy skills. It explains the process of learning to read and the response of the brain when exposed to text and music. It suggests a wealth of ideas to help parents and early years practitioners to support children's literacy learning.

Further information and downloadable resources can be found on the Sounds and Symbols website -

www.soundsandsymbols.co.uk

Sounds and Symbols also offers a business package for those wishing to present literacy-through-music sessions for pre-school children.

Aa Bb Cc
Dd Ee Ff Gg Hh
Ii Jj Kk Ll Mm
Nn Oo Pp Qq Rr
Ss Tt Uu Vv Ww
Xx Yy Zz

28203322R00031

Made in the USA
Charleston, SC
06 April 2014